Run

AF623575

Stephanie Pace

BookLeaf Publishing

Presentation by *BookLeaf Publishing*

Web: www.bookleafpub.com

E-mail: info@bookleafpub.com

ISBN: 9789357444941

First edition 2022

DEDICATION

To my mum who encouraged me to do this and listened to my ramblings and ridiculousness, helping me piece it all together.

Thank you to all those that supported me

ACKNOWLEDGEMENT

Thank you to all those that made this possible

PREFACE

I often find when I'm alone, the mind begins to wander and sometimes through the rambling and the wandering, a poem is born. So I wrote them down and this book was made. Enjoy the moments of a wandering mind

Run

Come on! Let's go!
We can be as free as wild stallions,
The wind lacing through our hair.

No time to waste! Don't stall!
We'll feel the ground rush beneath our feet,
No chain to hold us back.

Don't be afraid! We are free!
Our souls uncaged, eagles gracing the skies.
Our feet hardly touching the ground
What are you waiting for? Let's Run!

Tomorrow

A rancid orange sky
Like a heavy coat on fragile shoulders.
Is this the end?

A black choked ocean,
Thick like tar bubbling and bulging.
This can't be the end.

A mighty tower hollow and burnt.
A monument to greed laid to rest in rubble and rubbish.
This is the end, this is tomorrow.

The Chase

As pupils dilate and the skin prickles.
Blood turns to fire through the veins,
The heart dances with anticipation.

Blood pumping, teeth bared,
Ears like satellites pick up the adrenaline thick
in the air.

The thrill is in the chase,
Feet thump the earth, eyes fixed on their target.

A pounce ends it
Not with a bang but a whimper.
The thrill may be in the chase, but the reward is
in the capture.

Torn apart

I know I should go out,
Maybe just for coffee.
But that was our coffee shop.

Our friends invite me out on walks,
Just around that park with the lake.
But that's where I first kissed you.

You would probably tell me to get out of bed.
But I can't face rolling over and not seeing you.

It should be your tears I'm wiping at the altar.
You should be here not just as a photograph. My
world is a lot colder and darker without you in it.

An old friend

It's been days of trees and fields,
And it will be many more
Until I see that road sign.

Until I pass the shops on the corner, where I get my milk. I bet it's changed a lot since I was last there.

Until I pass my old school, I wonder if the toilet wall is still blackened.
If anyone asks, it wasn't me.

Until I hear that familiar squeaky gate,
The click of the key in the lock.
There are many more trees and fields.
Until I'm truly home.

That old tale

It's not my fault, I swear!
He swerved out in front of me,
I wouldn't tell a lie.

It's not my fault, officer!
He was speeding through a red light.
I'm innocent, I promise.

It's not my fault mum!
I tried to clean up my act, he crossed without looking, please believe me mum.

It's not my fault, your honor!
I didn't feel the drugs hit, I didn't mean to kill him, it wasn't my fault, it wasn't my fault.

Stolen years

I gaze at the mirror,
As it twists and cracks,
A thousand shards of your face.

The black tar from your heart,
Still bubbles and oozes
Over the place we laid.

That bitter cold in my soul
Is just an echo of the ice
That resides In yours.

The putrid stench of you hugs the walls, like a wretched tattoo,
Or an angry red scar.

Waiting on a war

Empty plates, bare cupboards,
In hungry, scrawny children
And overfed billionaires
Rider one is found.

Stone cold hatred and fear,
Pierce the silence with a Gatling gun.
In torn families and dead sons,
Rider two is seen.

Insatiable greed and demand
Poisons with power and the manic drive to
control, arrives rider number three.

As three unite the fourth
Not far now.
A consequence of the others,
Rider four is always one step away.

Thankyou

A red stain on a white dress,
You stole my beauty.
The broken bones you left me
Taught me to walk again.

Losing you left me burnt like a match,
But without you I'm the winner.
As I learn to run.

Thank you,
As I grace the skies proudly
It's because of you, that I learnt to fly

Open Doors

Through dark windows looking out
We sat and watched the days go by
Then week by week month by month.

We would listen to the children play
They'd giggle and scream it seemed like they
never ran out of games.

We'd bake and sleep, we'd decorate and
procrastinate. Although we shared some lovely
times. The doors are now open and the world
beckons.

Indiana

You greet me at the door,
You're always first to ask
Where I've been.

I cherish sunny days
Sitting in the sun just breathing in that
springtime breeze.

Though your fur grays, and joints ache
You never cease to remind me of those in your
life that make it all better

Long flights

Another airport, another flight,
Another safety brief of exits and I'm not sure
what I'm looking for in this

Off the plane in a daze,
Is today tomorrow or yesterday?
The brain is thick like fog with confusion.

Maybe I hope to find a piece I didn't know I had.
Or maybe I'm looking for my next conquest. All
I know is it grows,
Like an angry blaze it burns.

Friends to strangers

I was your shadow,
I wanted to share everything with you.
Back when I was young and clueless, but
nevertheless I was happy.

We shared common interests
And the same humor.
We were inseparable
And I loved you for all of it.

But just like that we grew apart.
We don't speak or laugh like we do. Instead we
work to erase any trace of each other's footprints
in our lives.

But you still exist in small ways.
You flitter through my thoughts. Like a distant
mirage. I know what I remember was only half
real.

Flawed logic

We are free to express,
Her skirt is too short,
She's asking for it.

Don't let them stop you living,
Out at night alone, a car in a bad neighborhood.
She's asking for it.

You only live once enjoy it
She was drunk and didn't say no
She was asking for it.

Get an education to thrive,
But her shoulders are exposed
She's asking for it.

Eagle dreaming

Come with me,
Brush those mountain tops
With the breeze of our wings.

Reach for the stars
The power behind us ever growing
We can fly forever.

With beauty and grace
We fly effortlessly
The patchwork quilt of green
Racing beneath us

Children of the earth

The seed so small
What big dreams await it?
What will it achieve?
Will it prosper? Will it thrive?

The sapling still so fragile
Grows slowly day by day.
The world around it is daunting and foreign.

A small tree now grips the earth
Among the mighty eucalyptus.
So far it's come and so far to go,
But it never stops reaching for the sun.

Potential beauty

Upon a naked canvas, potential hidden, waiting
eagerly for the artist.
Slashes of red and lines of black,
A layer of turmoil as the foundation.

Stripes of green and blue,
The purpose of the canvas is still concealed to
all but the artist.

Yellow flecks and pink speckles,
A dash of gray and a splatter of brown
The canvas is now complete, on display for all
the world to admire.

We Won't Sleep

Strip us down
Take our rights
Women's bodies now your property
But we won't sleep on this.

Control our bodies
Stunt our minds.
Make sure we are always complacent.
But we won't let this be.

We will pick up our banners
Hold our signs up
We will yell and scream and chant.
We won't sleep and neither will you

I want to live

You've seen my face on the news.
Afghanistan was taken over, homes and families burnt.

You've seen my face in the paper,
Hundreds killed in another military strike. They say this one had to happen. I don't know why.

You've seen my face on commercials
Pleading for aid. Begging for water and shelter.

You've seen my face, we want the same thing.
We want to live. We are all standing together,
one person won't help but we all can.

Electricity and water

I need you,
Like a toaster needs a bath
Like a mattress needs cement

I love you,
Like a ice loves fire
Like a spider loves a shoe.

I want you,
Like a lion wants a poacher
Like a tree wants an ax.

You are the orange juice to my toothpaste, it was so very nice to meet you, let's never meet again.

Spring

Swimming on lakes of honeydew
A blissful stroll beneath floral rain. Wrapped in a cardigan of sensory euphoria.

A melody of birds and bees feasting on the trees, the sun carrying worry away on golden waves. New life humming through the air.

www.ingramcontent.com/pod-product-compliance
Lightning Source LLC
Chambersburg PA
CBHW062110140826
49812CB00058B/1242
* 9 7 8 9 3 5 7 4 4 4 9 4 1 *